Grow
IN GRACE
& KNOWLEDGE

JAN VAN HEE

&

Sable Creek
PRESS

Cover and interior design by Diane King, www.dkingdesigner.com

All Scriptures are taken from the Authorized King James Version of the Bible.

ISBN: 978-0-9828875-6-1

Published by Sable Creek Press
PO Box 12217
Glendale, Arizona 85318
www.sablecreekpress.com

Printed in the United States of America

Dedication

To my husband Ron, under whose ministry of teaching and preaching I have learned so much from God's Word, and who encouraged and supported me in my writing, understood when dinner was a little late because I was "on a roll," and even helped out sometimes with the chores to give me time to write.

Contents

INTRODUCTION

This devotional journal is written for the purpose of helping you understand principles from God's Word that will help you live your Christian life in such a way that it will bring glory to God. If you will use it as intended, it will help you to not just read the devotional thoughts but to think upon them and personalize them.

HOW TO USE THIS DEVOTIONAL JOURNAL

- Read the devotional.
- Look up and read from your Bible all of the referenced scripture passages.
- Each journal page is divided into three topics: Praise, Prayer, and Project. Under each topic record praises, prayers and projects that come to mind in relation to the devotional subject. Thoughts are provided to get you started.
- Be sure you carry through with the projects you list.
- You may also want to think of a song or poem that is related to the subject.

1 Saved by Grace

"For by grace are ye saved through faith; and that not of yourselves: it is the gift of God: Not of works, lest any man should boast." Ephesians 2:8-9

Do you remember when you were in kindergarten or grade school and you planted a seed in a cup, set it in the sun, watered it and watched it grow? Remember how exciting it was when those first tiny green shoots appeared through the soil? You were observing the miracle of growth. The seed grew because it had life in it. But perhaps there were some seeds that did not grow. Why? Because they had no life; they were dead.

The Bible says in Ephesians 2:1 that until we trust Jesus Christ as our savior, we are "dead in trespasses and sins." We have no spiritual life. In the same chapter, verses four and five say, "But God, who is rich in mercy, for his great love wherewith he loved us, even when we were dead in sins, hath quickened us together with Christ, (by grace ye are saved)." The word "quickened" means "made alive." When we recognize our need of repenting (agreeing with God that we are sinners and then turning away from sin), and put our faith

and trust in Jesus Christ, God places within us his life—eternal life. Putting our faith in Jesus involves believing he died on the cross for us, paid the penalty for our sins, and rose again.

There is nothing we can do to deserve this life. It is a gift of God's grace. Ephesians 2:8-9 say, "For by grace are ye saved through faith; and that not of yourselves: it is the gift of God: Not of works, lest any man should boast." Grace in this instance has the idea of "unmerited favor." We do not deserve to have God love us, and we cannot earn the life he gives those who trust him. Titus 3:5 makes that clear: "Not by works of righteousness which we have done, but according to his mercy he saved us…" Jesus died in our place because he loved us even though our sinfulness made us unlovely. We just have to believe (trust or rely) in him, and he will give us the gift of spiritual life (John 3:16).

After we receive his life, God wants us to grow—just as you desired to see that little seed you planted grow. It is important to realize that no one can grow as a Christian until they have God's life dwelling within them. Many people "put the cart before the horse." They think that by doing good works and imitating the life of a Christian, they can become more like God and be accepted by him. They do not recognize that they cannot grow because they have no spiritual life. All of their good works mean nothing to God if they do not have a personal rela-tionship with him through Jesus Christ, his Son. Isaiah 64:6 says, "all our righteousnesses are as filthy rags."

As you begin this study, "Grow in Grace and Knowledge," examine your heart. Do you have spiritual life? Or are you just imi-tating the life of a Christian? If you have received God's eternal life by his grace, the following devotion-als will help you grow. If you have not received the Lord Jesus as your Savior, would you do it now?

TODAY'S PRAISE

I praise you and thank you, God, for the gift of eternal life.

TODAY'S PRAYER

Father, help me to appreciate the life you've given me and not to take it for granted. Help me to grow in grace and knowledge by studying these devotionals.

TODAY'S PROJECT

Find other scriptures which promise you eternal life. How can you share these scriptures with someone who does not have eternal life?

2 Growing

TODAY'S VERSE

"As newborn babes, desire the sincere milk of the word, that ye may grow thereby." 1 Peter 2:2

No words could describe the joy Mark and Angie felt when their precious, six-pound baby boy was placed in their arms. They were in their early forties and had given up hope of ever having a baby when Angie learned she was pregnant. Doctors said baby Adam was "perfect." But it soon became evident that he was not growing as quickly as he should, nor did he seem to make the "normal" responses mentally and emotionally. After months of testing and observation, the doctors determined that Adam's brain had not developed properly. He would never be able to grow and function like other children. In fact, doctors said he would probably never be able to function above the level of a three-year-old child, though his body would eventually reach adulthood. Mark and Angie were devastated. They loved Adam and did all they could for him, but each day of his life was a reminder of how limited his future would always be.

It is God's desire for his children to grow spiritually after he gives them new life. In Ephesians 4:15b we read that he wants us to "… grow up into him in all things, which is the head, even Christ." God wants us to grow up spiritually. Our goal in growing is to become a mature Christian by becoming like the Lord Jesus in our thoughts, actions and spirit. Verse thirteen of the same chapter says, "Till we all come in the unity of the faith, and of the knowledge of the Son of God, unto a perfect (mature) man, unto the measure of the stature of the fullness of Christ." Christ-likeness is to be our measure and our goal. Growing to be like Christ Jesus should be the norm for a believer in him. It must grieve him deeply when we do not grow as we should.

We must consistently expose ourselves to God's Word if we want to grow. Today's verse says, "As newborn babes, desire the sincere milk of the word, that ye may grow thereby." A baby begins life hungry for milk; we begin our Christian life by desiring the milk of God's Word—the "milk" meaning the things that are easier to understand. But as a child grows, he wants more to eat than just milk. As we grow in the Lord, we should desire and be able to understand the "meat" (harder things) of God's Word (Hebrews 5:12-14).

How much we grow depends a great deal upon us. God allows us to have a part in our spiritual growth. He supplies all we need for growth, but we must apply it to our life. His Word tells us in 2 Peter 1:3-4, "According as his divine power hath given unto us all things that pertain unto life and godliness, through the knowledge of him that hath called us to glory and virtue: Whereby are given unto us exceeding great and precious promises: that by these ye might be partakers of the divine nature, having escaped the corruption that is in the world through lust." We might say that after placing the "seed" of eternal life in us, God provides the "spiritual water" (his Word) and the "spiritual sunshine" (his love and grace). We must utilize them daily if we want to grow to spiritual maturity.

_____

_____

_____

_____

_____

_____

_____

_____

_____

_____

_____

_____

_____

_____

TODAY'S PRAISE

I praise you, Lord, for giving me everything I need to grow to a mature Christian.

TODAY'S PRAYER

Help me to not grieve you, Father, by not growing as I should.

TODAY'S PROJECT

Using God's Word as your measuring guide, examine your life. List areas where you know you are growing spiritually. Then list areas where you know you need to grow more Christ-like. Find verses to help you grow in those areas. Then with God's help START GROWING in those areas.

3 Grow IN Grace

"But grow in grace, and in the knowledge of our Lord and Saviour Jesus Christ. To him be glory both now and for ever." 2 Peter 3:18

Our theme verse tells us of two areas in which God wants us to grow. They are the basis for all other spiritual growth, and unless we are constantly developing in them, there will be no spiritual maturity. The first is grace; the second is the knowledge of the Lord Jesus Christ. Today we will consider what it means to grow in grace.

As we have already seen, "grace" in regard to salvation is God's unmerited favor toward us in forgiving our sins and freely giving us eternal life. For the believer, grace becomes the spiritual state in which we live and act. The idea of grace is further explained in Romans 5:1-2: "Therefore being justified by faith, we have peace with God through our Lord Jesus Christ: By whom also we have access by faith into this grace wherein we stand, and rejoice in hope of the glory of God." Peter also speaks of "the true grace of God wherein ye stand" in 1 Peter 5:12. This is the idea of grace in our verse today. This spiritual state is a gift of God; we do not deserve the privilege of living in it. It is a life of peace, knowing we have been accepted by him because of our faith in his Son (Ephesians1:6).

We are, however, responsible to grow in this state of grace wherein we live. We are not to remain a baby or to become stagnant. This is where grace takes on even a greater and more beautiful meaning. It includes the power and equipment God supplies to live the Christian life and to serve him. Paul speaks often in the Scriptures of the grace God gave him (and others) so that he could obey and serve the Lord. Look up the following verses: Romans 1:5; 12:6; 15:15; 1 Corinthians 3:10; Galatians 2:9; Ephesians 3:2, 7. Paul desired that the people in the church in Corinth have that same enabling grace as he says, "Grace be unto you, and peace, from God our Father, and from the Lord Jesus Christ" (1 Corinthians 1:3). In his letter to the church at Thessalonica he prays, "...that our God would count you worthy of this calling, and fulfil all the good pleasure of his goodness, and the work of faith with power: That the name of our Lord Jesus Christ may be glorified in you, and ye in him, according to the grace of our God and the Lord Jesus Christ" (2 Thessalonians 1:11-12).

It is clear God wants us to have his gift of enabling grace and that we are to grow in it. How do we do that? It starts with faith. Read 2 Peter 1:1-9. Here we find that we have obtained the same faith as the apostles and that God has given (and wants to multiply) grace and peace to us through the knowledge of him. In verse three he tells us he has given us everything we need that pertains to life and godliness. That means he has supplied grace to help us live for and serve him. He then gives us a list of characteristics we are to add to our faith. As we develop these things in our lives, we will be growing in grace. All we have to do is sincerely love God and be diligent in obeying him, and he will do the rest—by grace!

TODAY'S PRAISE

Think of a song or hymn that praises God for his grace and sing it to him. Two possible hymns would be "Amazing Grace" and "Grace Greater Than All Our Sin."

TODAY'S PRAYER

"Lord, make me mindful today of the ways you show me grace and the ways I need to grow in grace."

TODAY'S PROJECT

Starting with virtue, list seven things from 1 Peter 1 that you are to add to your faith. Then write beside each one how you can be more diligent in adding them. Try to find the time to find another verse about each one. Memorize verses to help in weak areas.

4 *Grow* IN KNOWLEDGE

TODAY'S VERSE

"But grow in grace, and in the knowledge of our Lord and Saviour Jesus Christ. To him be glory both now and for ever." 2 Peter 3:18

Today we will focus on the second part of our theme verse: "But grow…in the knowledge of our Lord and Savior Jesus Christ." The question has been asked through the ages, "How can man know God?" We must understand that we will never know anything about God through human intellect or reasoning. That would bring Him down to our level. We must remember the words of Deuteronomy 29:29, "The secret things belong unto the LORD our God: but those things which are revealed belong unto us and to our children for ever, that we may do all the words of this law." Though God created us with the need and capacity to know him personally, we can only know him as he chooses to reveal himself to us. Jesus said, "All things are delivered to me of my Father: and no man knoweth who the Son is, but the Father; and who the Father is, but the Son, and he to whom the Son will reveal him" (Luke 10:22). The Son, Jesus

Christ reveals the Father to us. Creation reveals that God exists and shows his power. God has also given us his Word, the Bible, to guide us into the knowledge of him. We must believe by faith that what Jesus and the Word reveal to us is all we need to know in this life.

God wants us to know him and have fellowship with him by knowing his Son and studying his Word. Read Colossians 1:8-9 where Paul prayed that the Christians would be filled with the knowledge of God's will in wisdom and understanding and that they would increase in the knowledge of God. Hosea 6:6 says, "For I desired mercy, and not sacrifice; and the knowledge of God more than burnt offerings." There is nothing you can do or give to God that would please him more than to know and love his Son. How well we know God will depend on how diligent we are in getting acquainted with his Son.

We get to know Jesus Christ in the same way we get to know

anyone else. We learn all we can about him and spend much time with him. Just spending a few minutes in Bible reading each day will not be sufficient to know and love him the way God desires. To really get to know someone, it is necessary to spend TIME with them…lots of time. We listen to their thoughts and share ours with them. The Bible is God's way of sharing his thoughts with us; prayer is how we express ours to God. God does not want us to just have a casual acquaintance with him. He wants us to LOVE him with all our heart. Bible study and prayer should not be a duty or drudgery; it should be our desire, our longing, because it helps us to know our Savior more intimately (Psalm 42:1-2). When God brings "Mr. Right" into your life and you find yourself "in love," you will feel like you never have enough time with this special young man, and you will want to know all you can about him. Should we not feel that way about our Savior who loves us more than any human ever could? We can spend our whole life getting to know him, and there will still be more to learn. God wants us to grow in our knowledge of his Son until we become like him (Ephesians 4:13).

TODAY'S PRAISE

I praise you, Lord, because you are a personal God who loves me and desires that I know you.

TODAY'S PRAYER

Lord, help me to desire to know you better. Show me more about you through your Word and through my relationship with your Son.

TODAY'S PROJECT

Figure out how much time you spend with a friend or someone else you love. How does that compare with the time you spend with the Lord? What do you plan to do to change that?

5 Grow in Faith

TODAY'S VERSE

"We are bound to thank God always for you, brethren, as it is meet, because that your faith growth exceedingly, and the charity of every one of you all toward each other aboundeth." 2 Thessalonians 1:3

I once received a gift of a necklace, comprised of a small glass ball (about the size of a small marble) hanging on a gold chain. Inside the ball was a tiny yellow seed which appeared to be about the size of a round pin head. Had it not been magnified by the glass, it would have looked smaller. It was a mustard seed. It's purpose was to remind me each time I wore it of Jesus' words in Matthew 17:20, "...If ye have faith as a grain of mustard seed, ye shall say unto this mountain, Remove hence to yonder place; and it shall remove; and nothing shall be impossible unto you."

The mustard seed in the little glass ball was a good reminder to have faith in God's promises, but it could never accomplish the purpose for which God created it while enclosed in the ball. God created it to grow. In Mark 4:31-32 Jesus says the mustard seed is the smallest of all seeds, "But when it is sown, it growth up, and becometh greater than all herbs, and shooteth out great branches; so that the fowls of the air may lodge under the shadow of it." Like the mustard seed, God wants our faith to grow. It took faith to trust God for salvation, but that faith needs to increase as we mature in our Christian walk. How do we grow our faith?

First, we must understand the true meaning of faith. Hebrews 11:1 says, "Now faith is the substance of things hoped for, the evidence of things not seen." Put simply, faith is believing what you can't see as if you could see it. Faith leaves no room for doubt. It involves total trust that God is who he is and that he not only can but will do what he promises. Sometimes that is difficult, and we must do as the father whose child was sick did in Mark 9:24. We must ask God to help us believe. The father prayed, "Lord, I believe; help thou mine unbelief." God will honor such a prayer.

Our faith will also grow as we get to know God better through studying his Word. Paul instructs Timothy to be "nourished up in the words of faith" (1 Timothy 4:6). We are also to build up ourselves on our faith (Jude 20). This has the idea of building through exercise or use. It is like an athlete building strength through physical training. The more we trust God and see him honor that faith, the more our faith will grow.

Lastly, our faith can grow as we observe the example of how God is honoring the faith of others. As you read about the great characters of the Bible, think about the faith it required on their part to be obedient and faithful to God and how God blessed their faith. Also observe the faith of Christians you read about or know. Paul exhorts Timothy "to be a good example of faith" (1 Timothy 4:6 & 12). Paul had been an example of faith to Timothy; then he encourages Timothy to be an example to others. Now it is your turn to grow your faith and be an example to others.

TODAY'S PRAISE

I praise you, Father, for giving the faith to trust the Lord Jesus as my Savior and that I can access that same faith to trust you in all areas of my life.

TODAY'S PRAYER

Father, increase my faith and help it to grow so that I can accomplish the purpose you have planned for me.

TODAY'S PROJECT

List the areas in your life where you need to grow in your faith. Can you find examples of people in the Bible or real life who needed faith in those same areas and whom God honored their faith?

6 DO YOU *Really* WANT TO KNOW *Jesus*?

TODAY'S VERSE

"That I may know him, and the power of his resurrection, and the fellowship of his sufferings, being made conformable unto his death; If by any means I might attain unto the resurrection of the dead." Philippians 3:10-11

Day four's devotional talked about how to know God. We learned that the only way to know God the Father is by knowing his Son, Jesus Christ. Many Christians are content with a very basic knowledge of Jesus. They seem to want to apply the first part of today's verse and skip to the last phrase so that it would read: "That I may know him and…attain unto the resurrection of the dead." They want to know Jesus just well enough to know that they have eternal life. How sad! The real joy of the Christian life is to know Jesus intimately, to identify with him—even being willing to suffer or die for his cause.

What does it mean to know "the power of his resurrection"? Do you remember what the disciples were doing after the crucifixion? They were cowering like frightened animals in a locked room. After seeing what happened to Jesus, they were undoubtedly fearful for their own lives. The book of Acts relates a different picture after Jesus rose from the dead and appeared to them in the upper room. No longer hiding, they were boldly proclaiming the story of Jesus and his resurrection to large crowds. What made the difference? Jesus' words in Acts 1:8 came to pass: "But ye shall receive power, after that the Holy Ghost is come upon you: and ye shall be witnesses unto me both in Jerusalem, and in all Judaea, and in Samaria, and unto the uttermost part of the earth." The Holy Spirit had come upon them, taken away their fear and given them power to share their faith. He also gave them power to serve God, to endure afflictions and to have hope, looking for the second coming of Christ. This was God's enabling grace.

Every Christian has the Holy Spirit abiding in his or her life and has access to that same kind of power. Ephesians 1:19 declares that believers can have this great power.

You may not be asked to stand before large crowds, but God wants each of us to be bold in our witness for him. It may be at school, on a sports team or at a community activity. It may be by going to the park with your youth group and sponsor to witness. It may be to give tracts to waitresses, clerks, or even the dentist. It might be sharing the gospel with a friend. God will give us power to serve him and live for him. There is no reason to be afraid of the task or say "I can't" because he will enable us to do things we never thought we could do (just as he did the disciples). Philippians 4:13 should be our motto: "I can do all things through Christ which strengtheneth me." If we do as Jesus commands, we will know his power.

Jesus' resurrection provided much more than just power over death and hell. It provided the Christian with the ability to live courageously for God and to boldly witness of our Savior. The question then is, "Do you really want to know the power of the Lord Jesus as his Holy Spirit makes it available to you? Or are you content to ignore the middle portion of today's verse?"

TODAY'S PRAISE

I praise you God that the Holy Spirit will give me power.

TODAY'S PRAYER

Lord Jesus, I want to know you more intimately by knowing your power in my life.

TODAY'S PROJECT

Purpose to let the Holy Spirit help you conquer your fear. Ask him to lay on your heart some way to serve God or to be a witness to someone this week. Spend time in prayer and then list what you need to do.

7 Whole OR Half?

TODAY'S VERSE

"And ye shall seek me, and find me, when ye shall search for me with all your heart." Jeremiah 29:13

Imagine how a young woman would feel if the young man she loved knelt before her and asked her to marry him saying, "I love you with part of my heart. I pledge half of my love to you and will share some of my earthly goods with you for a part of my life." How confident do you think she would feel that he really loved her? If she is wise, she will run the other way! Now, ask yourself how God must feel when we offer him the same kind of love and commitment.

The phrases "the whole heart" and "all thy heart" occur many times in the Bible. God makes it plain that he desires that we love him and serve him completely, totally committed to obeying him and pleasing him in every area of our life. Let's look at just a few of these areas.

God wants us to seek him with our whole heart. "With my whole heart have I sought thee: O let me not wander from thy commandments" (Psalm 119:10). "Blessed are they that keep his testimonies, and that seek him with the whole heart" (Psalm 119:2). These verses and our verse for today indicate that we are not to be half-hearted in seeking to know God. He promises that if we seek him with our whole heart, we will find him. We will enjoy not only his salvation, but a sweet, personal relationship with him if we daily seek him with our whole heart—in his Word, in prayer and in fellowship with him.

God wants us to pray with our whole heart. Psalm 119:58 and 145 emphasizes the importance of praying with our whole heart: "I entreated thy favour with my whole heart: be merciful unto me according to thy word" and "I cried with my whole heart; hear me, O LORD: I will keep thy statutes." This kind of praying would include sincerely confessing our sins, seeking to know God's will, asking for our needs, and interceding for others. Our little routine, insincere prayers have little power with God, but James 5:16 promises: "The effectual fervent (whole-hearted) prayer of a righteous man availeth (profits) much."

God wants us to praise him with our whole heart. Psalm 9:1 says, "I will praise thee, O LORD, with my whole heart; I will shew forth all thy marvellous works." In Psalm 111:1 we read, "Praise ye they LORD. I will praise the LORD with my whole heart, in the assembly of the upright, and in the congregation." We are to whole-heartedly praise God in and out of church. (Do you ever catch yourself thinking about something else while singing a familiar hymn instead of praising God by singing the words to him?)

God wants us to know and obey his Word with our whole heart. Did you notice how many of the above verses refer to God's Word? Psalm 119:34 says, "Give me understanding, and I shall keep thy law; yea, I shall observe it with my whole heart." God gets no pleasure out of seeing us learn his Word or obey him out of duty. He wants our whole heart! Does he have yours? Do you love him with all your heart, mind and soul (Matt. 22:37)?

TODAY'S PRAISE

I encourage you to think of your own list of things for which you can whole-heartedly praise God. You might want to start with his whole-hearted love for you.

TODAY'S PRAYER

What do you need to whole-heartedly talk to God about today? Perhaps ask him to forgive you for not seeking, praying, praising or learning and obeying his Word?

TODAY'S PROJECT

Look up Revelation 3:14-16 to see how God feels about those who are not whole-hearted in their love and service for Him. Can you find other Scriptures (use a concordance) that deal with the "whole heart" or "all thy heart"? Or perhaps songs with this idea that you can meditate on to help you love and serve God with all of your heart?

8 MAKING *Right* DECISIONS

TODAY'S VERSE

"For the LORD giveth wisdom: out of his mouth cometh knowledge and understanding." Proverbs 2:6

National newspapers carried the story of an eight-year-old boy who saved the life of his grandfather. The two were lobster fishing in the chilly waters off the coast of Maine when the grandfather was dragged into the water by a lobster trap rope and became entangled in it. The lad swiftly reached over the side of the boat and tied a life jacket around his grandfather who was barely conscious. Taking control of the boat, the boy circled the man until he spotted another boat and signaled it to come to their aid. When interviewed, the boy's father said the lad "kept his cool" and responded rightly "because he has been on fishing boats ever since he could walk." The lad knew what to do because he had been exposed to the sea, boats and experienced fishermen all of his life.

There is a lesson in this story. You may wonder if you will know how to make decisions and respond rightly in difficult or sudden situations. No one knows what tomorrow will bring, but how we respond to circumstances tomorrow depends on how familiar we get with God and his "way of life" today. If you consistently expose yourself to God's Word and learn from other godly Christians, then you, like the boy, will know instinctively what decisions to make and how to respond as you should.

How do you do this? Pay attention! If the boy had not paid attention, had he been playing or day dreaming instead of watching what the experienced fishermen did and listening to what they said, he would not have known what to do to save his grandfather. Many times, we do not really pay close attention to God's Word when it is taught or preached, or even when we read it ourselves. God frequently rebukes those who have ears but do not hear and apply his teachings. Read James 1:22-25 where he warns about this kind of attitude. He compares such indifferent hearing to one who looks in a mirror, notices something wrong, but walks away and forgets about it instead of following the correction of the mirror.

Study! 2 Timothy 2:15 tells us if we study God's Word, we will not need to be ashamed. We will make decisions that please God. Study requires time, effort and discipline. It implies learning and remembering, just as when you study for an exam. The word "approved" has the idea of "tested by trial." You will be tested, not on your knowledge, but on how you apply that knowledge by responding as God would have you to do when you are tried.

Pray for wisdom to make the decisions you need to make each day. God has promised wisdom as we need it. James 1:5 says, "If any of you lack wisdom, let him ask of God, that giveth to all men liberally…and it shall be given him." Wisdom increases as you pray for it and use it daily.

Seek godly counsel. Learn to ask for and seriously consider counsel from godly people. Proverbs 11:14 says, "Where no counsel is, the people fall: but in the multitude of counsellors there is safety." It is wise to learn from the experience and wisdom of those who have already traveled the path you are taking.

Today's Praise

I praise you, God, because you are Wisdom, and I thank you that you will share your wisdom with me.

Today's Prayer

Father, please give me wisdom to know your will. I especially need your wisdom in the areas of my life which I am listing.

Today's Project

List areas where you need God's wisdom. Be specific and ask especially for the ways you need it today. If you need godly counsel, write down the names of those you will ask to give it to you.

9 Consequences

"Be not deceived; God is not mocked: for whatsoever a man soweth, that shall he also reap." Galations 6:7

A good principle to hide in your heart would be, "You can choose your sin, but you can't choose the consequences." Sin always has consequences beyond our control.

We see this principle played out in chapters thirteen and fourteen of the book of Numbers. (Read these two chapters.) God was ready to move the Israelites into the land He promised them after the exodus from Egypt. Moses sent twelve men into the land to spy it out and bring a report back to him and the people. Though these spies saw amazing possibilities for blessing there, such as abundance of food, they also saw "giants" and possible obstacles. Conquering the land would involve battle and courage, but most of all it would require faith in God's promise to give them the land.

Ten of the men lacked such faith and tried to dissuade Moses from leading the people into the land. They caused the people to doubt God, to complain about their circumstances and to want to turn back to their old life. They refused to obey God and enter the land. Only two of the spies, Caleb and Joshua, had the faith to believe that God would do as he had promised and give them the land.

There were serious consequences to the choices the ten spies and the people made: (1) they were required to wander for forty more years in the wilderness, (2) the spies who discouraged the people died immediately, (3) there would be no military success in encounters with the inhabitants of the land, (4) no one who rebelled lived to see the promised land. The people were afraid that if they obeyed God, their children would fall prey to the enemy and die. Instead, the Israelites' disobedience cost them their own lives while their young children lived to enter the land forty years later. Their punishment would have been more severe if Moses had not interceded for them. Only Caleb and Joshua were honored for their faith and were allowed to eventually go into Canaan.

When the people saw their mistake, they decided to again disobey God and try to correct it on their own. They presumed to go fight against the Amalekites and the Canaanites and were defeated. They tried to change the outcome of their sin, but it was not possible. The Israelites had chosen their sin, but God chose their consequences.

God is a loving, merciful God who readily forgives sin when we are truly repentant. But that does not always change the consequences. He may forgive and give us a new direction, but sin always has consequences. Imagine hammering a nail into a board and pulling it out. A hole remains even though the nail is gone. Sin can be removed by God, but the principle of reaping the consequence of sin remains. What can we do when we sow sin? Sincerely ask God for forgiveness (1 John 1:9) and humbly submit to whatever consequence he allows. Things won't be the same as if you never disobeyed him, but God will forgive you, renew your joy and give you new direction. Good choices also have consequences. The Bible is full of God's promises to bless and do good to those who love and obey him. The choice is yours. The result of your choice belongs to God.

TODAY'S PRAISE

Thank you, Lord, for being willing to forgive me when I fail to trust you and obey you.

TODAY'S PRAYER

Dear God, help me to trust your promises and obey your direction. Help me to understand that though you will forgive me, I may still have consequences to face, and help me submit to them humbly.

TODAY'S PROJECT

List some of the times you have not obeyed God and the consequences that resulted.

10 Slave OR Servant?

"And whosoever will be chief among you, let him be your servant." Matthew 20:27

Christians sometimes talk about having a "servant's spirit." I wonder, however, how many really understand the biblical meaning of this expression. In our verse for today, as well as a number of verses that refer to the believer's role as a servant, the Greek word "doulos" is used. This word means "slave." In fact, "doulos" is the second most used word to describe Christians in the Greek New Testament manuscripts, occurring over one-hundred times. It is second to "disciples." The translators, however, most often changed it to "servant" (perhaps because it was more socially acceptable).

"Doulos" (slave) is the word Jesus used in our verse for today as well as in Mark 9:35 in teaching his disciples what their attitude should be toward others. It is also used in Matthew 25:21 when Jesus commended the faithful servant, and again in John 15:20 when he warns the disciples that they should expect to be treated the same as he was treated. It was the word Peter used in 1 Peter 2:16: "As free, and not using your liberty for a cloak of maliciousness, but as the servants of God." Paul said in 1 Corinthians 9:19: "…yet have I made myself servant (slave) unto all, that I might gain the more."

What difference does it make whether we think of ourselves as "slaves" or as "servants"? A slave is the property of his owner. His whole life is under the complete control of his master. He has no possessions, no rights or freedoms, and no will of his own. He is totally subject to his master. A servant is one who performs a service for his master but is not owned by him. He may have possessions of his own and make choices in areas not related to the service of his master. He may even choose to no longer be a servant.

Jesus wants us to voluntarily be slaves for God. He sets the example for us. Philippians 2:6-8 says: "Who, being in the form of God, thought it not robbery to be equal with God: But made himself of no reputation, and took upon him the form of a servant (slave), and was made in the likeness of men: And being found in fashion as a man, he humbled himself, and became obedient unto death, even the death of the cross." Jesus became a human slave in order to die on the cross and pay the penalty for our sins. As a slave he was humble and obedient to the Father. In John 5:30 he says, "I can of mine own self do nothing...because I seek not mine own will, but the will of the Father which hath sent me."

In Bible days, some slaves could earn their freedom after a certain period of time. Some, however, would choose to become bond slaves for life because they loved their master and wanted to continue to be his slave. Like them, and like Jesus, if we truly love God, we will submit our will to him and be willing to have a "slave's attitude," serving him in whatever way he chooses, expecting nothing in return. We will surrender all our possessions and all our rights to him. Verse five of Philippians 2 tells us, "Let this mind be in you, which was also in Christ Jesus."

TODAY'S PRAISE

Thank you, Lord Jesus, for becoming a slave for my sake.

TODAY'S PRAYER

Lord, help me to be willing to humble myself and have a "slave's attitude" in my service for you and others.

TODAY'S PROJECT

In what areas have you not had a "slave's attitude"? How do you plan to change that? Is there someone you need to apologize to for not having a humble, "slave's attitude" in how you have fulfilled obligations to them?

11 *God's* MATH

"And beside this, giving all diligence, add to your faith virtue; and to virtue knowledge; and to knowledge temperance; and to temperance patience; and to patience godliness; and to godliness brotherly kindness; and to brotherly kindness charity." 2 Peter 1:5-7

Math, like it or not, is an important part of life. A big percentage of daily living involves the use of mathematical facts. You can't even cook or sew or manage your money without a basic knowledge of math. We have, however, become so dependent on computers in our day that we rarely give much thought to addition or subtraction. Have you ever been in line at your favorite fast food restaurant when the computers go down? You are fortunate if the clerk can even figure how much change to give you.

Where did math originate? God is a God of order. He created the whole universe to have precise measurement in size, speed and operation. For example, if the sun and earth were only a few miles further apart or a few miles closer together, we would either freeze or burn up. Night, day, seasons, everything would be out of order and malfunction if God had not created them to operate by exact mathematical systems.

God also desires order and basic mathematical principles to be a part of our spiritual lives. Let's look at some of the subtractions and additions God expects us to do. First, consider some things we are to subtract. The Bible uses the words "put away" or "put off," but they convey the same idea as to subtract. Ephesians 4:22 tells us: "That ye put off concerning the former conversation the old man, which is corrupt according to the deceitful lusts."

The rest of that chapter contrasts the things we are to subtract from our lives and the things with which we are to replace them. Read the verses now, and write the things you are to subtract and their replacements in the project section of your journal page. Colossians 3:8-9 describes more of the traits of that old life-style: "But now ye also put off all these; anger, wrath, malice, blasphemy, filthy communication out of your mouth. Lie not one to another, seeing that ye have put off the old man with his deeds." Proverbs 4:24 admonishes us to, "Put away from thee a froward (deceitful) mouth, and perverse (devious) lips put far from thee." God wants us to subtract (take away, no longer to be considered as a part of the whole) anything that would identify us with our old sinful nature instead of with the Lord Jesus Christ.

Ephesians 4:24 and Colossians 3:10 point out that when you trust Christ as Savior, you "put on" (add) the new man. Verses 11-17 of Colossians 3 identify more characteristics of the new man which we are to add to our life. Write them in the project section. Our verses for today also list seven things we are to add. We need to daily do our "spiritual math homework" to be sure we are adding and subtracting according to God's directions in his text book, the Bible.

God is clear that there is an area where we are NOT to add or subtract. We are forbidden to add to or to take away from God's words. Read Deuteronomy 4:2, 12:32 and Revelation 22:18. God will not hold the person guiltless who does so.

TODAY'S PRAISE

I praise you, Lord, for how perfectly and precisely you created all things.

TODAY'S PRAYER

Father, help me to appreciate the importance of "spiritual mathematics." Help me to do my "spiritual homework" in subtraction and addition and to do it well, with diligence.

TODAY'S PROJECT

You should have done this as you read the devotional; if not, do it now. Can you add to the lists during the week?

12 *Gifts* AND *Talents*

TODAY'S VERSE

"For I say, through the grace given unto me, to every man that is among you, not to think of himself more highly than he ought to think; but to think soberly, according as God hath dealt to every man the measure of faith."
Romans 12:3

What do you think of when you hear the word "gift" or "talent?" Perhaps you think of someone who can play the piano flawlessly or sing beautifully or paint lovely landscapes. There are many kinds of gifts and talents. "Gifts" in the Bible speak of special abilities God gives each Christian to use to benefit other believers, while talents are the natural abilities we already have at birth. It may be that you look at other people's gifts and talents and feel that you have none. The truth is that God has blessed each of us with some special gift or talent. However, because we tend to compare ourselves to others, which God says in 2 Corinthians 10:12 is unwise, we often fail to recognize our gifts and talents and use them properly. We may discredit them or not use them at all. We might even take the credit for them and become proud or boastful.

Read the twelfth chapter of Romans. After urging us to present our bodies to God as a living sacrifice and to have our minds transformed in order to prove what is the good, acceptable and perfect will of God, Paul speaks of how we are to view the gifts God gives us. We learn in verse 3 that we are not to think of ourselves more highly than we should but to think soberly (seriously). We are to recognize that our abilities come from God and not become proud because we have them. James 1:17 tells us that "every good gift and every perfect gift is from above, and cometh down from the Father." We did nothing to get or create the gifts we have. God gave them to us. If we are wise, we will work hard to develop and properly use them, but we had nothing to do with their origin.

Romans 12:4-6 tells us that just as a body has many different parts, each of which has its own purpose, each of us has different gifts and talents. Wouldn't it be boring if we all had the exact same gift or talent? The next few verses list seven ministry gifts and explain the attitude with which they are to be used.

- Prophecy: delivery of God's Word, to be done according to faith
- Ministry: service to others
- Teaching: instructing others with the Word
- Exhortation: encouraging, comforting, and sometimes admonishing others
- Giving: sharing what one has, to be done simply and without pretense
- Ruling: leadership ability, to be done diligently
- Mercy: sensitivity and acts to benefit others, to be done cheerfully

These few ministry gifts are by no means all the gifts and talents God gives, but it would be good to consider if you have any of them.

The important principle to keep in mind is that you should discern your gifts and talents. Humbly receive them as from God and use them to benefit others (especially those in the body of Christ) and to bring honor to God.

TODAY'S PRAISE

Thank you, Father, for the special gifts and talents you have given to me to use for your glory.

TODAY'S PRAYER

Please help me to develop my gifts and show me how you want me to use them.

TODAY'S PROJECT

Make a list of your spiritual gifts and your other talents. Use Romans chapter twelve as a guide. You may want to ask an adult what talents and gifts they think you have. Beside each one, write a way you can use it to serve God and be a blessing to others.

13 Running THE Race

"Wherefore seeing we also are compassed about with so great a cloud of witnesses, let us lay aside every weight, and the sin which doth so easily beset us, and let us run with patience the race that is set before us…"
Hebrews 12:1

A stunned world watched during the 2010 Winter Olympics in Vancouver, Canada, as the coach of a speed skater, far ahead of his competition, waved the skater into an "illegal" lane, causing him to lose the gold medal. The coach had become confused and signaled the athlete over too soon. It didn't matter. It was an illegal move and cost the young man his coveted gold.

Paul sometimes used athletic terms in describing the life of a Christian. On three occasions he compares the Christian life to a race. In 2 Timothy 2:5, he no doubt has the Grecian Olympics in mind as he says, "And if a man also strive for masteries, yet is he not crowned, except he strive lawfully." It didn't matter if the runner came in first. If the rules were not followed, he was disqualified. Almost everything in life has rules or regulations one must heed if they expect to be a winner. Not heeding these rules, intentionally or not, usually means disqualification and loss of the "crown" or prize. It is important to study the rule book and know the rules before starting the race. We must be students of God's Word to learn God's expectations of us as we run our race of life.

Running a race requires having a goal. Paul speaks of running a race in 1 Corinthians 9:24 -27. In verse 26 he says he is not running his race "as uncertainly" (without a goal).We must run to reach the goal and obtain the prize, determined to win. Paul reminds us in verses 24 and 25 that we are not running to obtain a corruptible (earthly) crown or reward, but are striving for an incorruptible one that will last for all of eternity. The word "strive" indicates the extreme effort required to do this.

Discipline is necessary in preparing for the race. Athletes have strict rules regarding the care of their bodies when they are training for a race. They have to deny them-selves many things to be healthy and in good condition. They learn to discipline and control their bodies (verse 27). Why? They don't want to be a "castaway" (one who is disapproved or disqualified). Hebrews 12:1 speaks more of this training. We are to "lay aside every weight, and the sin which doth so easily beset us." When training, athletes often wear weights which they remove for the real race. We cannot run a race cumbered down with weights. We must lay aside everything that would keep us from running the best we can.

We must run with patience. A runner runs the race one step at a time but each step is necessary to reach the finish line. We must live our Christian life one day at a time, striving to do our best each day. Hebrews 12:2 tells us to keep our eyes on Jesus as we run. Only God knows when we will cross the finish line, and it is his "Well done" we want to hear as we com-plete our race.

TODAY'S PRAISE

What a wonderful trainer and coach the Holy Spirit is as I run my life race. He will never point me to the wrong lane. And how thankful I am for the clear instruction given in God's Word so that I know how to run.

TODAY'S PRAYER

Father, help me to run my race with patience and to keep my eyes on Jesus as I run.

TODAY'S PROJECT

Determine what "weights" in your life might be keeping you from running your race the best you can. List them and determine to lay them aside.

14 *Everybody* ELSE"

"And be not conformed to this world: but be ye transformed by the renewing of your mind, that ye may prove what is that good, and acceptable, and perfect, will of God." Romans 12:2

"But, Mom, everybody else is going" (or "doing it" or "getting it")! Do those words sound even vaguely familiar? Chances are that you or one of your friends has used them in an effort to persuade parents to come around to your way of thinking. Most humans are sociable beings. We want to be liked and to be accepted, especially by our peers. Somehow that translates in our thinking to being like "everybody else." If our friends or social groups are going somewhere or doing something or possessing something we don't have, we often feel the need to be like them. We don't want to be left out and be "different." That is very faulty thinking for a Christian.

God created each of us uniquely different. If he had not wanted us to appreciate our differences, he would have made us all alike—same looks, same abilities, same way of thinking and expressing ourselves. How boring that would be! The Bible says in Psalm 139:14a, "I will praise thee; for I am fearfully and wonderfully made." The surrounding verses tell how even our members (body parts) were fashioned by God. Each of us is a "fashion original." God made us to please him! We are special to him. May we be grateful we are who we are and not try to be like "everybody else," not even other Christians.

God's people are supposed to be different and separate from the people of the world. Being like the world displeases God and brings heartache and problems. Let's look at the Children of Israel as an example. God faithfully delivered them from slavery in Egypt, provided for their needs, helped them win battles and led them to a land of "milk and honey." He repeatedly warned them that when they came to the Promised Land, they were not to become like the inhabitants. They were not to marry them nor worship their gods. He also warned them of the consequences if they did so. He used prophets and judges to teach and guide them, but he was their King and Ruler. They needed no other. After a while they were discontent with God as their king and said to the prophet Samuel: "Now make us a king to judge us like all the nations" (1 Samuel 8:5). Samuel went to God with the problem. God told him to warn them of the consequences: the king would take their sons and daughters for his soldiers and servants; he would take their fields and land and work animals; he would take a percentage of their crops and livestock. Yet they insisted they wanted to be like the nations around them. God gave them their desire. How they eventually would regret their decision (1 Samuel 8).

It has always been God's will for His people to be separate and different from those of the world. We should want to be like Jesus, to be identified as God's children and have no desire to be like the unsaved people around us. Nor do we need to be like other Christians, especially if they are not totally living for God. Read 1 John 2:15-17 and Romans 8:29. It is okay to be different if you are what God wants you to be.

TODAY'S PRAISE

I praise God for making me unique and special. I am thankful I am not like "everybody else."

TODAY'S PRAYER

Lord, help me to be content with who I am, including my looks, my personality traits, my family, my financial circumstances and even the restrictions you have placed in my life.

TODAY'S PROJECT

List areas in your life where you may have wanted to be like "everybody else." Put some thought into why God may not want you to be like others in these areas.

15 *Things*

"Let your conversation (life-style) be without covetousness; and be content with such things as ye have: for he hath said, I will never leave thee, nor forsake thee." Hebrews 13:5

In today's world, happiness is often equated with possessions. Everywhere you turn, you are confronted with some form of advertisement urging you to buy something. Many people, even Christians, are obsessed with money and what it can buy. Christian teens put pressure upon their parents to buy them the newest computer or electronic gadget, the most popular brand of clothing or the latest form of entertainment. Moms and dads sacrifice precious time with their families in order to earn more money to provide their families with more things.

This love of money brings to mind the literary character Silas Marner who, because of ill treatment from the village people, moved to an isolated place and became an introverted miser. His sole delight became hoarding and counting his gold coins each evening as he ate his meager meal. Until one night, his only love, his gold, was stolen. There was noth-ing left in his life except misery as his only joy was gone. He then sat each night by the fire holding his head and moaning. Of course, the moral of the story is that money cannot bring true happiness.

Jesus warned against materialism (Luke 12:15-34). In verse 15 Jesus said, "Take heed, and beware of covetousness: for a man's life consisteth not in the abundance of the things which he possesseth." He then tells of the rich man who hoarded his possessions but lost his soul. What good did the man's possessions do him then? Jesus proceeds to teach his disciples that they are not to focus upon even the daily necessities of life such as food and clothes because their Heavenly Father knows their need and will take care of them. He tells them to seek God's kingdom (spiritual things), and God will take care of their needs (Matthew 6:33). To live with such a mind-set requires faith. It also requires that we make a choice to love God more than we love the things of this world. 1 John

2:15 tells us, "Love not the world, neither the things that are in the world. If any man love the world, the love of the Father is not in him." Verse seventeen goes on to say, "And the world passeth away, and the lust thereof: but he that doeth the will of God abideth for ever."

"Things" will not last. But when we put God first, He will not only give us eternal life but also treasures in heaven.

1 Timothy 6:5-10 warns that those who want to be rich fall into temptation, a snare and many hurtful lusts. Verse ten points out that the love of money is the root of all evil. There are those who believe the more you possess, the more "spiritual" you are, but Paul says we should withdraw from those that think gain is godliness. Is it wrong then to have money or possessions? Not if God has blessed you with them. But riches are not meant to be used for your own selfish enjoyment. 1 Timothy 6:17-19 says that those who are rich are to use their riches to do good and to share with those in need. The secret to a proper view of "things" lies in today's verse. Read it again thoughtfully.

TODAY'S PRAISE

I praise God that He knows my needs and has promised to supply them.

TODAY'S PRAYER

Dear Father, forgive me for the times I have been covetous. Teach me to be content and grateful for what you have given me and to realize that is all I need.

TODAY'S PROJECT

Keep a record this week of every time you say: "I want…" or "I wish …" or "I need …" or some similar statement. Then ask, "Is it a legitimate need or am I being covetous?"

16 THE GREEN-EYED *Monster*

TODAY'S VERSE

"For where envying and strife is, there is confusion and every evil work."
James 3:16

We often confuse envy and jealousy. To be jealous implies that one is watchful or guarded over what he or she feels is rightfully his or hers. It is possible to be jealous in a good way. For example the Bible speaks of God as being jealous over his people. Exodus 34:14 says, "For thou shalt worship no other god: for the LORD, whose name is Jealous, is a jealous God." God has every right to be guarded and protective of his people. He wants them to be faithful to him and not to follow false gods. There may also be appropriate times for human beings to be jealous. A mother certainly has a right to be guarded and protective over her children. The problem is that we humans have a tendency to let our jealousy get out of control and turn to anger, resentfulness and malice toward other people because of real or perceived rights. For instance, a teen girl may have a crush on a boy and "stake her claim" on him. He doesn't really belong to her, but she becomes hateful toward every other girl who may even talk to him. Or she may have gotten a new outfit to wear to a special event or church, and guess what? Susie Q shows up with one just like it. She becomes jealous because she thinks no one else has a right to wear "her" outfit.

To be envious is to be discontent and have ill will because of the advantages and possessions of another person. It is never good and usually causes great harm. Think about it. Why did Cain kill Abel? He was envious over the fact that God accepted Abel's offering because Abel had obeyed God and made the sacrifice God required. Why did Joseph's brothers sell him into slavery? They were envious of the special favor their father showed Joseph and the dreams God gave him. Ananias and Sapphira died because they were envious of the recognition Barnabas had received for giving his all to the Lord. They wanted the same praise, so they lied to the Holy Ghost by lying to the church. King Ahab became depressed, pouted and was angry because he was envious of Naboth's vineyard. God took his life also. (You can read these stories in Genesis 4:1-15, Genesis 37, Acts 5:1-11 and 1 Kings 21:1-26).

Envy is not only disastrous to the person who is envious, but it may (can) harm many other people. Reread today's verse. Where there is envy there is every evil work. The Bible encourages us, "Let us walk honestly, as in the day...not in strife and envying" (Romans 13:13). Envying is one of the works of the flesh listed in Galatians 5:19-21. We are told not to walk (live) in it. It is truly a "green-eyed monster" which will destroy everything in its path.

We can avoid envy by recognizing and dealing with its causes: (1) being discontent with what God has given you; (2) comparing yourself to others. We have already discussed number one. Remember that Hebrews 13:5 tells us to be content with such things as we have. 2 Corinthians 10:12 says those who measure and compare themselves to others are not wise. If you feel envious or jealous in a wrong way, remind yourself of these principles. Don't let the "green-eyed monster" destroy you or anyone else.

TODAY'S PRAISE

Thank you, God, that you are jealous over me because you love me and want to guard and protect me.

TODAY'S PRAYER

Lord, it is so easy to be envious of others. Please help me not to be envious.

TODAY'S PROJECT

If you are envious or wrongfully jealous of someone or some "thing," write down the name of that person or thing. Also write why you are envious. Now, list a blessing you have that could help you be content instead of envious. Do this for every area in which you are envious or jealous.

17 OTHERS' *Things*

"Look not every man on his own things, but every man also on the things of others." Philippians 2:4

If you have ever watched preschoolers at play, you have observed one of the basic problems of humankind—selfishness. Occasionally there will be a child who seems to be naturally tender-hearted who would rather share than cause another child grief, but for the most part, sharing and thinking of the needs of others is something a child must be taught. We are all by nature sinful, selfish beings.

However, the child of God, who has been saved by his grace and has his Spirit dwelling in her life, should manifest the unselfish character of God. She should not selfishly think of herself, her needs and her desires, but should think of others and their needs and desires. The context surrounding our verse for today talks about having the same kind of mind (thinking) toward others that the Lord Jesus had. Verses six through eight remind us that though Jesus was in the form of God and equal with God the Father, he gave up his rights as God, took on a human body and became a servant. He even humbled himself to the point that he died on the cross. Why? Because he loved us. We were more important to him than his own rights. Can you even imagine what it must have been like for God the Son who had all power with no limitations, all the glory and beauty of Heaven and the sweet fellowship of his Father, to give that all up to be confined to a human body and come to live in a world that was wicked, among people who despised him? Philippians 2:3 tells us, "…but in lowliness of mind let each esteem other better than themselves." The only way we can do this is to learn to see and love others like the Lord Jesus does.

Manifesting an unselfish character also involves having a proper view of ourselves. Just as a little child must learn that life is about more than just her, we must understand that life is not all about us. This is contrary to the philosophy of the world which constantly bombards us with such slogans as, "You deserve the best," or "You are worth it," or "You must fight for what you want." God's Word says just the opposite. Consider these Scriptures: "Even as I please all men in all things, not seeking mine own profit, but the profit of many, that they may be saved" (1 Corinthians 10:33); "We then that are strong ought to bear the infirmities of the weak, and not to please ourselves" (Romans 15:1); "Bear ye one another's burdens, and so fulfil the law of Christ" (Galatians 6:2); "Let no man seek his own, but every man another's wealth" (1 Corinthians 10:24).

These verses all indicate that we are to put the welfare of others before ourselves, whether that be spiritual, physical or material. And this does not mean we get to be selective in whom we treat this way. Sometimes it is easier to put our best friend first than it is to put our parents or siblings before ourselves. Aren't you glad that God wasn't selective in deciding whom he would love and for whom Christ Jesus would die? Christ died for everyone! If you have not developed unselfishness in your life, it may take some effort and time. But with God's help, you can learn to esteem others better than yourself.

TODAY'S PRAISE

I am so thankful that Jesus loved me enough to put me before his own rights as God the Son.

TODAY'S PRAYER

Lord, help me to put others before myself. Forgive me, and show me where I fail in this.

TODAY'S PROJECT

If you have been selfish in not putting others first, write down goals and ways to change this (specific people you need to consider and ways to put them first).

18 THE *Grace* OF *Giving*

TODAY'S VERSE

"…remember the words of the Lord Jesus, how he said, It is more blessed to give than to receive." Acts 20:35b

Do you remember the meaning of the word "grace"? With regard to salvation, grace is God's unmerited favor in choosing to forgive our sins and give us the gift of eternal life through his Son, Jesus Christ. For a Christian, grace is that enabling power God gives us to live for him and do his will. Sometimes the result of this power is also called "grace." This is the case in the context of 2 Corinthians 8 and 9 where Paul refers to giving as "this grace." Note especially 2 Corinthians 8:7 & 19. The grace Paul is talking about was a special offering the church had collected and was sending to help the persecuted Christians in Jerusalem. God enabled the believers in Corinth, even those who were themselves experiencing trials and deep poverty (verse 2), to give to others in need.

Giving is a vital part of Christian character. God is a giver; his greatest gift was his Son. If we are to manifest the character of God in our lives, we must learn to be givers. To have the right attitude toward giving, we must understand that it is by God's grace that we have anything to give. James 1:17 tells us, "Every good gift and every perfect gift is from above, and cometh down from the Father of lights." We must also understand that God desires that we first give our heart and life to him. Look at 2 Corinthians 8:3-5. These believers "first gave their own selves to the Lord." If you have not given yourself completely to God, it is unlikely you will give your possessions to him.

Giving can be divided into two main categories: tithes and offerings. The word tithe simply means "one tenth" of what you possess or gain. The Old Testament makes it clear that we are to give back to God a tithe of all he gives us. There is no evidence this changed in the New Testament. In fact, Jesus emphasizes the importance of tithing in Luke 11:42 when he tells the Pharisees that they should tithe on even the small things, but they should not pass over judgment (right) and the love of God. All other forms of giving are types of offerings. These may include giving extra to God's work (church projects, missionaries, etc.), giving to meet someone's need (the poor, the sick, the persecuted, etc.) or a love gift (something given out of love just to be a blessing or encouragement).

Attitude is most importance when we give. We should give to God and others because we love God and want to please him. God honors our giving, not according to how much we give, but according to our heart attitude when we give. Remember the story in Mark 12:41-44 of the poor widow and the rich men? Jesus said the widow gave more with her little "penny" than all the rich men together. Why? Because she gave sacrificially from a heart of love. 1 Corinthians 13:3 tells us, "...though I bestow all my goods to feed the poor...and have not charity (love), it profiteth me nothing." We learn in 2 Corinthians 9:7, "Every man according as he purposeth in his heart, so let him give; not grudgingly, or of necessity: for God loveth a cheerful giver." If you want to experience great joy, develop the grace of giving in your life!

TODAY'S PRAISE

I praise You, Lord, that you are the Giver of life and of salvation.

TODAY'S PRAYER

Father, help me learn to be a loving, unselfish giver.

TODAY'S PROJECT

Examine your giving. Have you given yourself to God? Do you consider your possessions (money and things) to belong to you or to God? Would you give them away if God asked you to do so? What is your attitude in giving? What can you do to become more like God in your giving?

19 *Curiosity* AND THE *Cat*

TODAY'S VERSE

"Be sober, be vigilant; because your adversary the devil, as a roaring lion, walketh about, seeking whom he may devour." 1 Peter 5:8

In an upscale neighborhood near the foothills on the edge of Salt Lake City, Utah, some children saw what they thought was a large cat bound across yards and jump into the window well of a house. Being curious, they followed it and peered down into the well. Upon seeing how large the "cat" was, they ran to tell their father who went to investigate and discovered a cougar from the nearby Wasatch Mountains. The father notified proper authorities who tranquilized and returned the animal to the mountains.

Without knowing it, the children's curiosity endangered their lives. Instead of following the cougar, they should have realized it was no ordinary cat and informed an adult. The outcome could have been much different for them.

The Bible tells us that Satan, "as a roaring lion, walketh about, seeking whom he may devour." Like the children, we often fail to recognize him or understand how dangerous he can be. We see him

as only a large "cat" and allow our curiosity to place us in possible danger. The temptations he lays out before us seem harmless and even fun. Before we realize what has happened, he ensnares us. To avoid this, we must grow in our knowledge of our enemy. 2 Corinthians 2:11 says, "Lest Satan should get an advantage of us: for we are not ignorant of his devices."

We are to "stand against the wiles of the devil" (Ephesians 6:11). "Wiles" are methods Satan uses to lure and trap us. We know from God's Word that Satan is a liar and deceiver and that he can transform himself into an "angel of light" (John 8:44 and 2 Corinthians 11:14). We can conclude, therefore, that his methods will be tricky and appealing. They can even appear to be something good. Satan can only be in one place at a time, but he has followers and methods everywhere who take great pleasure in defeating Christians and destroying the lost. This is why you must be sober (serious minded) and vigilant in dealing with him. He is not a joke. He is your constant enemy, and you must always be watching out for ways he will beguile you. You must learn to recognize your enemy, avoid his snares and depend upon God for help.

We are also told in Ephesians 6:11 to "Put on the whole armour of God, that ye may be able to stand against the wiles of the devil." Listed as armor are the girdle (belt) of truth, the breastplate righteousness, footwear with the preparation of the gospel of peace, the shield of faith, the helmet of salvation, the sword of the Spirit (God's Word)

and prayer (Ephesians 6:14-18). All of these are necessary to withstand the devil. Leaving off even one makes you vulnerable to Satan's attacks. If we are vigilant, we don't need to worry. James 4:7 tells us to "Submit yourselves therefore to God. Resist the devil, and he will flee from you."

Our protection against falling for Satan's "wiles" comes from three things: (1) putting on the whole armor of God, (2) submitting yourself to God, (3) resisting the devil. If we do these things, the devil will flee from us. The victory will be ours!

TODAY'S PRAISE

I am thankful, Dear God, that you have given me all I need to withstand Satan and his wiles. Thank you that I can have victory!

TODAY'S PRAYER

Father, teach me to be alert and vigilant in recognizing Satan's wiles and snares. Help me to be serious about avoiding them.

TODAY'S PROJECT

List some of the areas in your life where Satan has tricked you and caused you to sin in the past. What can you do to be more serious and vigilant to avoid these same snares?

20 Sleeping *Christians*

"Therefore let us not sleep, as do others; but let us watch and be sober."
1 Thessalonians 5:6

Isn't it strange how when you go to bed at night, it seems like one minute you are awake and the next it is morning? God created us with a need for rest, and he gave our body the ability to restore itself through sleep. At the end of a busy day, we look forward to crawling into bed, closing our eyes and sleeping. It is definitely something good.

But sometimes sleep can be dangerous. One church will probably never forget the Sunday when part way through the sermon, they heard a loud crash about half way back in the pews. Every head turned to see a grown man picking himself up from the floor. After working a night shift, he had hurried home, cleaned up and dutifully gone to church. But his weary body, used to sleeping at that hour, yielded to sleep and crashed to the floor with a loud thud during the service. An embarrassing moment indeed!

There is a similar story in the Bible in Acts 20:7-12. Paul was preaching to the church in Troas. Apparently it was a very long message for verse seven says he "continued in his speech until midnight." The church was meeting in a large, third-story room. People sat wherever they could find a spot. One young man chose to sit on the ledge of an open window. As it got late, he fell asleep and tumbled from the window, plummeting to the ground below. He appeared to be dead. Upon reaching the young man, Paul said, "Trouble not yourselves; for his life is in him." Bible scholars differ as to whether the young man was dead and Paul, through the power of the Lord Jesus, restored life to him or whether he was only seriously injured, appearing dead, and Paul healed him. Either way, it was a miracle, and there was great rejoicing.

It can be dangerous to literally fall asleep in church, but it is also dangerous to fall asleep spiritually. There are a number of ways a Christian can be asleep when she should be awake. First, the Bible often admonishes us to "hear" the Word of God. That means to pay close attention to and to apply it to our lives. How many times have you sat in church or read the Scriptures and not really paid attention nor applied it to your life? How often we are like the disciples of whom Jesus asked in Mark 8:18: "…and having ears, hear ye not? And do ye not remember?" We often fail to really hear God's Word.

We can also sleep when we should be watching and praying. The disciples were guilty of this. Read Luke 22:39-46. At a time when they would soon face great trial and needed prayer desperately, they fell asleep. They should have been watching, which means to be alert or vigilant, and praying for strength to overcome the coming temptations. Our verse for today tells us we need to watch and to be sober (serious minded). Some Christians sleep when they should be looking for the return of the Lord Jesus. Read Mark 14:34-37. Not a day should pass that we do not look for his coming. Lastly, we sleep when we should be serving Jesus and witnessing for him (Mark 16:15). It is time to "…awake out of sleep" (Romans 13:11).

TODAY'S PRAISE

I praise you, God, that you never slumber nor sleep, but are always awake and aware of me and my needs (Psalm 121: 3-4).

TODAY'S PRAYER

Father, I realize that there are times I have been spiritually asleep. I confess them now to you and ask forgiveness. Help me to stay awake in spiritual things.

TODAY'S PROJECT

What are some specific ways you need to be awake spiritually? List areas where you want to purpose to do better. If you can take the time, you might also want to find examples, especially in the book of Proverbs, where God disapproves of sleeping at the wrong time; then make spiritual applications to your life.

21 BECOMING A *Gracious* WOMAN

TODAY'S VERSE

"A gracious woman retaineth honour." Proverbs 11:16

What is a gracious woman? The word "gracious" comes from the same root word as grace and has several meanings. Usually when used in the Bible, it is speaking of God's grace and kindness toward man. Psalm 86:15 says, "But thou, O Lord, are a God full of compassion, and gracious, longsuffering, and plenteous in mercy and truth." In our verse for today, however, it refers to a particular character trait belonging to a woman and emphasizes a benefit of being gracious. The word "retaineth" means to lay hold of as a support. Thus, a gracious woman will hold tightly to her honor (which implies a reputation which adheres to a keen sense of right and wrong and conducting oneself in a pure and dignified manner). Such a reputation will be valuable to her as a means of protection and influence. This is why the rest of the verse compares her to a man who is able to use his finances for the same purpose. A man uses his business skills to gain influence. A gracious woman's honor will gain her the same power.

An important trait of a gracious woman is kindness. Kindness is an inner quality which is displayed by a sympathetic, friendly nature and by gentle, tender-hearted, generous acts. This is the part of God's character which is referred to when the Bible speaks of him as gracious. One favorite verse regarding God's kindness is Isaiah 54:10: "For the mountains shall depart, and the hills be removed; but my kindness shall not depart from thee, neither shall the covenant of my peace be removed, saith the LORD that hath mercy on thee." This verse points out the enduring, steadfastness of God's kindness. It never changes. A gracious woman will also be consistent in her kindness. It will not be something she "puts on" like a garment when it is convenient, but an ingrained part of her character with which she will respond in every circumstance in life. It will motivate her to acts of kindness toward others, endeavoring to be a blessing to them.

A gracious woman is kind to everyone…even her enemies.

Jesus says in Luke 6:35 that just as God is kind to the unthankful, we are to love our enemies. The previous verses clarify how we are to respond to those who mistreat us. Read verses 27-36. This is only possible if we learn to be more concerned about others than about ourselves and learn to be sensitive to their needs. Instead of responding in anger when we feel someone mistreats us, we need to respond with kindness.

A gracious woman is identified by her speech. This is a trait for which the ideal woman in Proverbs 31 is praised. Verse 26 tells us: "She openeth her mouth with wisdom; and in her tongue is the law of kindness." Colossians 4:6 says, "Let your speech be alway with grace, seasoned with salt, that ye may know how ye ought to answer every man." You will never be known as a gracious woman if hateful, mean, ugly, belittling words come out of your mouth or if you lie or gossip. Remember that what comes out of our mouth comes from our heart (Luke 6:45). The only way gracious words can come out of our mouth is if we have a sweet, kind heart. Are you becoming a gracious woman? Not if you are not cultivating kindness in your heart. God commands, "And be ye kind one to another…" (Ephesians 4:32).

TODAY'S PRAISE

I praise you, Lord, for being so kind and gracious to me. Some of the ways I see you kindness toward me are:

TODAY'S PRAYER

Father, help me to be more gracious in my heart and to display the trait of graciousness (kindness) in how I think, act and speak.

TODAY'S PROJECT

In what areas of your life do you need to be more gracious? List these areas, and one by one start working on being more gracious. Or, if you feel you have already developed the trait of graciousness, can you think of ways to expand and demonstrate kindness to others?

22 Is It *True*, Kind, and *Necessary?*

"For my mouth shall speak truth; and wickedness is an abomination to my lips. All the words of my mouth are in righteousness; there is nothing froward or perverse in them." Proverbs 8:7-8

Socrates, an ancient Grecian philosopher, was once approached by an acquaintance who wanted to share some information about a mutual friend. Socrates responded by saying he would first like to put the information through a triple filter test. He said, "The first filter is truth. Have you made absolutely sure that what you are about to say is true?"

"Well, no," the man said, "I just heard about it."

Socrates replied, "So you don't know if it is true or not. Let us try the second filter, the filter of goodness. Is what you are about to tell me about my friend something good?"

The man replied, "No, on the contrary…"

Socrates said, "You want to tell me something bad about my friend, but you're not certain if it is true. You may still pass the test, however, because there is one filter left, the filter of usefulness. Is what you want to tell me about my friend going to be useful to me?"

"Not really," the man answered. "Well," concluded Socrates, "if what you want to tell me is neither true, nor good, nor even useful, why tell it to me at all?"

The dictionary describes a "gossip" as one who chatters or repeats idle talk and rumors about others. The word itself is not in the Bible, but there are a number of other words which mean the same thing and which God warns us against. The first one is in the Ten Commandments. "Thou shalt not bear false witness against thy neighbor" (Exodus 20:16). God forbids us to say anything about another person that is not true, and Proverbs 6:19 tells us it is one of the things God hates. Thus, it is our responsibility to be absolutely sure that what we say concerning another person is factual. Ephesians 4:15 says, "But speaking the truth in love…" We are not only to speak the truth at all times, but we are to do so in love. It is not loving to tell an untruth about someone!

Ephesians 4:31 lists five things

a Christian is to "put away." Evil speaking is one of those things. Proverbs 16:27-28 says, "An ungodly man diggeth up evil: and in his lips there is as a burning fire. A froward man soweth strife: and a whisperer separateth chief friends." Where does gossip originate? Isn't it usually from someone who wants to hurt another person and chooses speaking evil of them as his or her method to do so? Gossip is a powerful tool for hurting others. Proverbs 18:8 says, "The words of a talebearer are as wounds, and they go down into the innermost parts of the belly." Verse 21 of the same chapter says, "Death and life are in the power of the tongue."

Certainly, a Christian should not want to be part of such wicked destruction!

Not even the truth always needs to be repeated. Proverbs 12:23 tells us, "A prudent man concealeth knowledge: but the heart of fools proclaimeth foolishness." Proverbs 11:13 reminds us, "A talebearer revealeth secrets: but he that is of a faithful spirit concealeth the matter." A Christian should never be guilty of repeating idle talk or spreading rumors. A good safeguard would be to ask yourself before you listen to or repeat anything: "Is it true? Is it kind? Is it necessary?"

TODAY'S PRAISE

I praise you, Father, that you have given me your Word and your Spirit to guide me in my speech.

TODAY'S PRAYER

Father, please help me to remember before I speak to ask the questions: "Is it true? Is it kind? Is it necessary?"

TODAY'S PROJECT

Look up these additional Scriptures and examine your speech in light of them. Proverbs 4:24; 5:2; 6:17,19; Proverbs 8:6-9; 9:13; 10:8,10,11,18-21, 32-32; 11:9,11,13; Proverbs 12:17-19,22-23,25: 14:5; 15:2,7,14,28; Proverbs 16:21,23-24, 27-30; 17:4, 27-28; 18:6-7,13,20-21; Proverbs 19:5; 20:19; 21:23,28; 24;28-29; Proverbs 25:3-24; 26:19-28. (It will only take a few minutes). Write down whatever corrections you need to make in your speech.

23 "I'm *Sorry*"

TODAY'S VERSE

"If we confess our sins, he is faithful and just to forgive us our sins, and to cleanse us from all unrighteousness." 1 John 1:9

An article entitled "The Five Most Difficult Things to Say" listed the words "I'm sorry" as number one. Why is it so hard to admit we are wrong and to offer an apology? Our pride wants us to defend our actions, to minimize our fault and to shift blame to others. Read the story of Adam and Eve and the serpent in Genesis chapter three, noting especially verses 9-13. Adam and Eve both knew God's command not to eat of the tree of the knowledge of good and evil, but what happened when God confronted them with their disobedience? Adam blamed Eve, and Eve blamed the serpent. They were not willing to acknowledge and be accountable for their sin. God, however, held both of them responsible for their own sin and each had consequences to suffer as a result.

One of the best things you will ever learn to do is to be honest about and acknowledge your sin. To do so, you need to understand that God expects more than a quick, insincere "I'm sorry." God wants us to be heartbroken over our sins. After David had sinned with Bathsheba and had her husband killed in battle, he poured out his heart to God in prayer for forgiveness. In Psalm 51:1-3, he confessed his sin and pleaded for God's mercy and forgiveness. He said, "For I acknowledge my transgressions and my sin is ever before me." In verse four he recognized that though he harmed others, his primary offence was against God, for he had violated God's rules. Then in verse seventeen he said, "The sacrifices of God are a broken spirit: a broken and contrite heart, O God, thou wilt not despise." All sin is against God. It should break our hearts when our actions, thoughts, disobedience or lack of love for God cause him grief.

God also expects us to truly repent. What is repentance? The biblical meaning of repentance is to feel such regret or dissatisfaction over something that you change your mind and your ways. It has the idea of turning around and going in the opposite direction. Real repentance is not just feeling remorseful over your sin, but being so disturbed by it that you turn away from it and begin to do whatever is necessary to avoid doing it again. Many people claim to be sorry for their sin and say, "I'm sorry" but go right back to that same sin. That is not what God wants. Paul speaks of this in 2 Corinthians 7:9-10 when he says, "Now I rejoice, not that ye were made sorry, but that ye sorrowed to repentance: for ye were made sorry after a godly manner…For godly sorrow worketh repentance to salvation not to be repented of: but the sorrow of the world worketh death."

Repentance is absolutely necessary for salvation! It is also necessary in the life of a Christian. We are not without sin. We must learn to acknowledge our sin, truly sorrow over it and repent of it, turning away from it.

The penalty for our sins was paid by Jesus on the cross. However, because we still have our sin nature, we still sin. But our loving, merciful God promises us that "If we confess our sins, he is faithful and just to forgive us our sins, and to cleanse us from all unrighteousness."

TODAY'S PRAISE

I praise you, God, because Jesus paid for my sins on the cross and because when I sin as a Christian, you forgive and cleanse me.

TODAY'S PRAYER

I pray I will listen to the Holy Spirit when he convicts me of sin and will promptly, sincerely ask forgiveness with the determination to truly repent. (If you are aware of sins you need to confess, do it now).

TODAY'S PROJECT

Today's lesson focused on saying "I'm sorry" to God. But God wants us to also ask forgiveness of other people we have wronged (James 5:16). Do you need to ask forgiveness of someone? If so write down his or her name(s). Figure out the best way to apologize sincerely and specifically for your fault without putting any of the blame on the other person.

24 *Hold* My Hand

TODAY'S VERSE

"Fear thou not; for I am with thee: be not dismayed; for I am thy God: I will strengthen thee; yea, I will help thee; yea, I will uphold thee with the right hand of my righteousness." Isaiah 41:10

Five-year-old Timmy insisted on taking the lead when he and his sisters, ages three and six, would walk to the park with their grandmother. "I am the only man, so I should lead," he would assert boldly. He stopped at every street crossing and made sure it was safe for the others to cross. One day, however, while passing a house where a new family had recently moved in, a growling, barking Doberman greeted Timmy as he walked by the chain-link fence on the side of the yard. The dog jumped at the fence and showed his teeth. Timmy stood petrified for a moment until his grandmother caught up with him, and they all walked quickly away from the yard. On the way home, Timmy again took the lead, but as he approached the house with the dog, he hurried to his grandmother's side, put his hand in hers and said, "Grandma, hold my hand to home." The point of this illustration is that even leaders are sometimes afraid and find comfort in holding the hand of someone else.

Holding hands has always been a way of showing affection for someone, of comforting and encouraging and of giving a sense of security. Sometimes clasping of hands is for the purpose of giving strength or aid to another. Do you remember reaching for the hand of your mom or dad when you were afraid or insecure or needed to feel their strength or comfort? Now that you are older, you may not feel that need so much, but there are times when it is still comforting to have someone hold your hand. Is God's "hand" the first you reach for at such times?

Even though the Bible tells us that God is a spirit and does not have a body (John 4:24), it sometimes describes God as having physical features. This helps us understand God in a more personal way and visualize his relationship with man. A number of verses mention God's "hand." Read the following verses: Psalm 17:7;

Psalm 20:6; Job 12:8-9; Ecclesiastes 9:1; and Isaiah 59:1.

Our verse for today reminds us that God will hold our hand in times of need. He assures us that we need not fear because he is with us. We need not be dismayed or overwhelmed because he is our God. He promises to strengthen and help us. Then he sweetly promises to uphold us with his right hand. Look at verse thirteen of the same chapter, "For I the LORD thy God will hold thy right hand, saying unto thee, Fear not; I will help thee." Picture it! For two people to hold each other's right hand they have to either be face to face or standing very close to each other. God, both the Almighty One and our Loving Father, will hold our right hand with his right hand! He is that close when we have a need. All we have to do is by faith put our hand in his (even though we can't see it) and say, "Father, hold my hand to home."

_____

_____

_____

_____

_____

_____

_____

_____

_____

_____

_____

_____

_____

_____

_____

_____

_____

Today's Praise

God will hold my hand in times of need.

Today's Prayer

Lord, help me to remember to reach out for your "hand" and sustaining grace when I have a need instead of being afraid or trying to deal with the problem myself.

Today's Project

If you have a hymnal which contains the song "He Holds My Hand," read or sing the words. If not, create your own song or poem about God holding your hand.

25 *Living* IN TROUBLED *Times*

TODAY'S VERSE

"And we know that all things work together for good to them that love God, to them who are the called according to his purpose." Romans 8:28

Every teen would like to grow up in untroubled, peaceful times. But history proves few teens have had that privilege. Today we are living in tough times. TV, radio and newspapers bombard us with news of a bad economy, wars, world conflicts, crime and acts of gross immorality. Christians in some parts of the world are suffering severe persecution, and Christians in America are facing more and more opposition. Such times can be stressful for teens. A teen may sometimes feel fearful and wonder what her future holds. How do you live in troubled times without becoming discouraged and feeling hopeless?

As with all of life's challenges, the answer is in the Word of God. There we have instructions to just keep trusting in God, knowing that all he allows in our life is for our spiritual benefit and his glory (Romans 8:28). There we find examples of people who lived in troubled times, such as Job, Joseph, Moses, Daniel, Esther, the early Christians and disciples, and the Apostle Paul. Each faced different but difficult trials in troubled times. Job lost his possessions, his children and even his health. To make it worse, his wife and his "friends" mocked and discredited him. Joseph's family did not understand him and ridiculed him, and his brothers sold him into slavery in a foreign land. He was tempted, lied about and forgotten in prison, but he lived such a godly life that he was eventually promoted to great honor and saved his people from starvation. Moses, Daniel and his three Hebrew companions, and Esther all lived under oppression in countries that had conquered their people. Yet, they continued to trust the true and living God and weren't afraid to share their faith in him. Even today, Christians in many parts of the world are suffering for their faith. God gives them the courage they need to do so.

These believers would not turn their backs on God no matter how difficult the circumstances. Daniel 1:8 says, "But Daniel purposed in his heart that he would not defile himself…" The first step in staying true to God is to purpose in your heart that you will not be defiled by the world and ungodliness…no matter what. Think ahead of time how you plan to respond in various situations where you might be tempted to be defiled.

Understand that in this life you will have tribulations and maybe even persecution (John 16:33). Believe that God is Faithful and will give you the ability and strength to stay true to him in every situation. Read 1 Corinthians 10:13. He does not promise to remove the trial, but he will help you through it. Remember Romans 8:28. Life is like a puzzle in which each piece is revealed only as it is needed. But God designed the whole puzzle and knows exactly how each piece fits. Trust him to put it together (Proverbs 3:5-6). In the book of Philippians, from a dirty dungeon, Paul often speaks of joy and reminds the believer to "rejoice." Following many persecutions he commands in 1 Thessalonians 5:18, "In (not for) everything give thanks." Remember, Jesus will never leave you nor forsake you… good times or bad (Hebrews 13:5).

TODAY'S PRAISE

I praise you, God, that you are always with those who trust in you and will be with them through every trial.

TODAY'S PRAYER

Father, like men and women in the Bible who stayed true to you in troubled times, may I also be faithful to you no matter what my circumstances.

TODAY'S PROJECT

Choose one of the Bible characters mentioned in today's devotion and read about them in your Bible. Make a list of ways they lived in troubled times, and under each trial, write how they responded to it. Then meditate upon why they were able to respond as they did.

26 Grace TO Suffer

TODAY'S VERSE

"Let us therefore come boldly unto the throne of grace, that we may obtain mercy, and find grace to help in time of need." Hebrews 4:16

Suffering is not something we like to think about, especially when we are young. It is important, however, that Christian teens have a proper, biblical perspective of suffering because you will at some time either experience it yourself or watch someone you love suffer. Undoubtedly, some of you already have.

Suffering comes in many different forms. It may come as physical affliction or mental stress. It may be the result of emotional or spiritual pressures. It can be caused by outward trials and even persecution. Often the first reaction a person has to suffering is to ask, "Why is this happening to me?" The implication of this question is, "Why me…instead of someone else?" A better question might be, "Why not me?" Suffering is the byproduct of sin. Adam and Eve's disobedience to God brought sin into this world, resulting in not only every evil deed imaginable but also in grief, sorrow and suffering. We must understand that suffering is

a "normal" part of life and that it falls upon Christians the same as anyone else. The difference for the Christian is that God will give us "grace to help in the time of need" (today's verse), so when trials and suffering come, instead of bewailing our lot and asking "Why me?" we need to go to God and ask for his grace to deal with the need. The Bible is full of assurances that God will be with us in times of trials and suffering.

The next question often asked is, "What did I do wrong to deserve this?" This is a valid question, especially if the person asking it has been walking in disobedience to God. God does sometimes use suffering to chasten his children when they stubbornly refuse to live as he asks. Read Hebrews 12:5-11. God's chastening is always done in love. But not all suffering is the result of sin or disobedience. Once, the disciples asked Jesus why a man was blind. Was it because he sinned or his parents had sinned? Jesus replied, "Neither hath this man sinned, nor his parents: but that the works of God should be made manifest in him" (John 9:1-3). In this situation, Jesus healed the man, and many believed on Jesus. On the other hand, the apostle Paul suffered from a physical affliction (possibly an awful eye disease) which God did not choose to heal. Read 2 Corinthians 12:7-12. Instead, God told Paul, "My grace is sufficient for thee: for my strength is made perfect in weakness." God used Paul's suffering to teach him dependence upon God's grace and to keep him humble. In both cases suffering pointed others to God and brought him glory.

Paul's reaction was to rejoice in his suffering. This is the way a Christian should respond even in persecution. Many Christians around the world are persecuted for their faith. They accept persecution joyfully because Jesus said, "Blessed are ye, when men shall revile you, and persecute you, and shall say all manner of evil against you falsely, for my sake. Rejoice, and be exceeding glad: for great is your reward in heaven" (Matthew 5:11-12). What matters is not "why" we suffer, but "how" we respond to the suffering that comes our way. Will we access God's grace for help and use suffering for his glory?

_____
_____
_____
_____
_____
_____
_____
_____
_____
_____
_____
_____
_____
_____
_____
_____

TODAY'S PRAISE

I praise you, Lord, because you allow me to come to your throne of grace to find help in times of suffering.

TODAY'S PRAYER

Lord, forgive me if I have whined about the suffering in my life or in the life of someone I love. Help me to see suffering as a normal part of life, and help me find ways to point others to you in how I respond to suffering.

TODAY'S PROJECT

First find promises in God's Word that can help and encourage you (or others) in times of suffering. Secondly, if you know someone who is suffering, think of a way to be a blessing to them.

27 ARE YOU *Prepared*?

TODAY'S VERSE

"Therefore be ye also ready: for in such an hour as ye think not the Son of man cometh." Matthew 24:44

A tragic thing happened in our community recently. Three teenagers decided to drive to the top of a nearby mountain to view the city lights at night from a lofty advantage. The young man who was driving was not familiar with the dirt road and thought he was turning onto another dirt road. Instead he drove the car off an embankment. He and the two young ladies were wearing seatbelts and were able to undo them and crawl out of the car. Usually it would have been wise to stay with the car and to wait for help, but they were in a place where no one would see them; besides, the likelihood of someone else being on that road at night was slim, and they had no cell phone service. So they started walking. They were, however, shook up and disorientated...and cold! In this part of the country, the temperatures can drop below freezing very quickly. Exhausted, they decided to crawl up in a somewhat sheltered place to rest. The young man told the two girls to sleep, and he would stay awake and watch over them. When the girls awoke a few hours later, they found that the young man had also fallen asleep. They woke him and helped him to his feet, but after a few steps he collapsed and died from hypothermia. The girls walked on until they found help.

These were good kids, and they were doing nothing wrong, but they had failed to prepare. First, they had told no one where they were going. Secondly, only one girl had a coat of any kind which she shared with the other girl as they slept huddled together and which probably saved their lives. The young man had nothing to help keep him warm.

Have you run out the door without a coat or in some way failed to be prepared for some unforeseen circumstance? We have all done it, not only physically but spiritually. This reminds us of the parables of the five foolish virgins and of the unprofitable servant in Matthew 25. Read verses 1-30. The virgins knew the bridegroom was coming; they just didn't know when. They should have always been prepared by having their lamps filled with oil. And the servant, knowing what kind of businessman his master was, should have handled his talent (money) more wisely. In other words, they should have been prepared.

There are several areas in the Christian life where God says we need to be "ready" (equipped or prepared). We are to prepare to withstand evil. Ephesians 6:13 says: "…and having done all, to stand." Daily put on the whole armor of God in order to withstand evil.

Timothy is told to be prepared to help others (1 Timothy 6:18) and Titus to be ready to do good works (Titus 3:1). 1 Peter 3:15 tells us, "…and be ready always to give an answer to every man that asketh you a reason of the hope that is in you with meekness and fear." Paul was prepared to suffer and die for Christ (Acts 21:13). And, we are to be ready when Jesus comes again (Matthew 24:44). Don't face any of these events unprepared. Prepare your heart and mind by growing in the grace and knowledge of the Lord Jesus Christ. Live as if he were coming today. He might!

TODAY'S PRAISE

I praise you, Lord, that I don't have to face life's challenges unprepared because you have given me your Word to prepare me.

TODAY'S PRAYER

Help me, Lord, to learn to prepare my heart and mind so I can withstand evil and be obedient in every area of my life. (Are there specific areas of your life you need to ask God's help in being more prepared)?

TODAY'S PROJECT

List some instances in your life where you have not been spiritually prepared when they happened. Find Scriptures that will help you be prepared in these areas the next time you are confronted with them. (Examples: not knowing what to say when you have an opportunity to witness or a sin you yielded to when you were tempted).

28 *God* SEES

TODAY'S VERSE

"For his eyes are upon the ways of man, and he seeth all his goings." Job 34:21

In Genesis chapter 16 we have the story of how complicated and sad people's lives can become when they step outside the will of God. When he called Abraham (Abram) to leave his home in Ur, God promised he would make a great nation from him. Since God established marriage at the time of creation as a means of procreation and Sarah (Sarai) was Abram's wife, God intended that this great nation come from the two of them. But after many years of being unable to have a child, Sarah became impatient and persuaded Abram to take her Egyptian handmaid, Hagar, and have a child with her.

Hagar had no choice in the matter. She was a slave with no rights of her own. She had to do as her mistress and master ordered. Her child would not even be considered her own but rather Abraham and Sarah's.

Of course, under such circumstances, trouble broke out in the home. The young handmaid began to despise her mistress. Perhaps she was proud that she was going to bear Abraham a child when Sarah could not. Perhaps she was angry because the child would not rightfully be hers. Perhaps she felt she ought to be treated with more respect since she was performing such an important service for her master and mistress. Her motives are not revealed, but the result was that Sarah became angry with Hagar and blamed Abraham for the situation. Abraham wanted no part in the feud and gave Sarah permission to do whatever she wanted with Hagar. We don't know what Sarah did to Hagar. The Bible only says, "And when Sarai dealt hardly with her, she fled from her face" (Genesis 16:6).

Verse seven says, "And the angel of the LORD found her by a fountain of water in the wilderness." Can you picture a young woman sitting by the fountain weeping? Can you imagine how frightened and desperate she must have felt? She was with child through no fault of her own. She didn't know where to go or what to do next. Returning to her mistress might mean punishment or death, but wandering in the wilderness could also mean death for her and her child. She possibly did not even know where she was. But the LORD knew where she was; he knew everything about the situation. He sent an angel to confront her and instruct her regarding her future. The angel told her to go back to her mistress and submit to her. He also promised to make another nation from her son. Hagar's response was that "…she called the name of the LORD that spake unto her, Thou God seest me"

(Genesis 16:13). The Hebrew word for this expression is El roi, literally meaning "God is seeing." God continued to see and protect Hagar as she returned to her mistress.

The people in this story made bad choices and stepped out of God's will, but he did not forsake them. He saw their need and met it. Seven times the Gospel of John notes that "Jesus saw." Each time he responded to the need of those he saw. God sees you. He knows your needs. He will meet those needs if you come to him for help.

TODAY'S PRAISE

Thank you, Lord, for never letting me out of your sight. Thank you for always seeing and meeting my needs.

TODAY'S PRAYER

Lord, help me to so live that you will be pleased with all you see in my life.

TODAY'S PROJECT

Read Psalm 139 and list all the ways and places this psalm applies to God's knowledge of you.

29 What About *Tomorrow*?

Today's Verse

"Boast not thyself of tomorrow; for thou knowest not what a day may bring forth." Proverbs 27:1

People have a tendency to put a lot of hope in "tomorrow," a day which has not yet come. Perhaps you have heard such expressions as "It will be better tomorrow" or "My dreams will all come true tomorrow." People seem to feel that "tomorrow" belongs to them, and they can mold it to suit their own desires. Let's look at some principles from God's Word regarding "tomorrow."

The concept of tomorrow can be divided into three areas: (1) literally the day after today, (2) any time in the future in this life and (3) the future in Eternity. What does God have to say regarding these three "tomorrows"?

Proverbs 27:1 says, "Boast not thyself of tomorrow; for thou knowest not what a day may bring forth." This could mean the next day or a future time. This brings to mind the rich man in the New Testament. Read Luke 12:13-21. He was proud of his riches and made plans to possess even more. Meanwhile, he would relax and enjoy his wealth. But Jesus said he was a fool. Why? Because he did not acknowledge God's rightful ownership not only of all he possessed but of his soul. He had no place in his scheme of things for God! God told the rich man he would die that night. What good would his treasures be to him then? This philosophy is also spoken of in Isaiah 56:11-12 (read) where those who were supposed to be shepherds for God had become greedy and thought, "… and tomorrow shall be as this day, and much more abundant." No one has a guarantee of tomorrow on this earth. How wise we would be to prepare for the "tomorrow" of Eternity!

The Christian should view "tomorrow" on earth with an entirely different perspective. First, keep in mind that you must consider God's will in every tomorrow. Look at James 4:13-15. According to this passage, our plans ought to be made with the understanding that we might not have a tomorrow. Therefore, we submit our plans to God's will and say, "If the Lord will, we shall live, and do this, or that." To leave God out of our plans is evil. We must pray and seek God's will for each future activity and not just go ahead and make our plans expecting God to then bless them.

A Christian should not be worried about tomorrow. After telling us how he takes care of the birds, flowers, grass and the animals, God reminds us that he knows our needs. If we put him first, he will provide for us (Matthew 6:25-34). Verse 34 says, "Take therefore no thought for the morrow: for the morrow shall take thought for the things of itself." This does not mean we are not to be wise and make plans according to God's will. It means we trust God, knowing he loves us and will care for us.

Non-believers may realize life is short and have the attitude mentioned in 1 Corinthians 15:32. Read this passage. They know they are going to die, but instead of preparing to meet God, they decide to "live it up." A Christian looks forward to a future based on God's promises for all eternity. We KNOW we will spend "tomorrow" with God!

TODAY'S PRAISE

I am so thankful God will be with me and meet my needs for every tomorrow.

TODAY'S PRAYER

Lord, help me remember to seek you in all my plans for all my tomorrows.

TODAY'S PROJECT

What future plans have you made? List them. Did you remember to check them out with God first? You might want to write a poem or song or just a list about how you can depend on God for your tomorrows.

30 CAN "JUST ONE" MAKE A *Difference*?

TODAY'S VERSE

"I can do all things through Christ which strengtheneth me." Philippians 3:13

A teenage girl approached me after I spoke at a Ladies/Teens meeting and asked, "Do you really believe a teenager can make a difference?"

I answered with an emphatic "Absolutely!"

Maybe you wonder the same thing about yourself, "Can I really make a difference?" or "Who am I that my life should matter for the cause of Christ?"

Let us look at some Bible examples where "just one" made a difference. Consider Esther who was probably still a teen when, because of her beauty, she was chosen to be among the harem of women who would be considered as the future queen of Persia. Who would have thought a humble Jewish girl—not a Persian, not from royalty or position—would be chosen as queen? But she did much more. Because of her courage and her willingness to risk her life for God, she saved her whole nation (which was subject to Persia) from annihilation. One young woman made a difference! Read more in the book of Esther.

Daniel and his three friends were among many young people who were captured and trained to be servants of the king of Babylon, but it seems that only they had the courage to stand by the scriptural standards they had been taught and the courage to voice them to their captors. Daniel seems to have been the strongest in his faith and was the spokesman for the others. Because of his obedience and walk with God, he was able to interpret the king's dreams and was eventually promoted to the office of first president of the land. God also used him to provide prophecy regarding the future, including some yet to come. One young person made a difference. Read more in the book of Daniel.

Then there was the immoral Samaritan woman who was living in sin. She met Jesus at the well, believed in him and went back to her village telling others about him. Because of her witness, the Bible says many believed on him (John 4). Her story reminds me of a teen revival meeting my husband preached in a little Kansas town. The youth group was small with only about fifteen teens who all attended public school. During the week, my husband told them that he was going to preach on Hell the last night and urged them to bring their friends. On the final night the church was packed with teens. At the close of the service, thirty-five young people accepted Jesus Christ as their Savior. One girl had become burdened for her peers in her school and with God's help, persuaded them to come to the meeting. Because of one girl, many put their faith in Christ, and that school and that church, even that town was changed!

There are many examples in the Bible and in history where one person made a difference. You may be thinking, "But they were special." No, they were just like you. The thing that made them different so that they could make a difference in the world was their faith in and obedience to God. God wants to use each of us to make a difference in the lives of others in some way. It is up to us to seek to know his will as to how he wants to use us and then to be obedient to that will. We need to believe our verse for today as well as Mark 9:23. You can absolutely make a difference!

Today's Praise

I praise you, Father, that you can use me to make a difference!

Today's Prayer

Lord, help me to be willing to be that one who makes a difference for the cause of Christ.

Today's Project

Today's project is two-fold. Make a list of individuals who have made a difference in your life. Make a second list of people you can think of that you can make a difference in their lives at this time. (Hint: a friend or family member who doesn't know Christ as Savior? Someone who could use your encouragement or help in some way? A child or another teen you could be an example to)?

31 *Living* THE ABUNDANT *Life*

TODAY'S VERSE

"...I am come that they might have life, and that they might have it more abundantly." John 10:10b

Hollywood and the media like to portray the Christian life as dull, unexciting and full of drudgery. Not So! The Christian life, if lived rightly, is a life which abounds with joy, excitement, adventure and more. The life God gives us when we accept Jesus as Savior is "abundant," (very plentiful, more than sufficient). It comes from the same root word as "abound" which has the idea of full and overflowing. Let us look at a few of the "abundant" blessings God gives a Christian.

Joy—In John 15:11, Jesus said, "These things have I spoken unto you, that my joy might remain in you, and that your joy might be full." The joy God gives is "packed down and running over." No temporary "happiness" offered by the world can match it. Christian young people are usually the most joyful young people in the world. Even when going through trials, the Christian can have an inner joy.

Hope and Peace—Romans 15:13: "Now the God of hope fill you with all joy and peace in believing, that ye may abound in hope, through the power of the Holy Ghost." Many teens today are without hope. The circumstances of their lives make the future look hopeless. Many have no peace, no inner tranquility. Their lives are full of mental and emotional turmoil. This is evidenced by soaring numbers of teen suicides as well as drug and alcohol addictions and high crime rates among teens. Christian teens, on the other hand, can have an inner peace, knowing that God loves them, is watching over them and will allow only those things in their lives that are for their good. They have a hope (which in the Bible means a confident assurance) of eternal life and of God's guidance in this life.

Love—1 Thessalonians 3:12: "And the Lord make you to increase and abound in love one toward another, and toward all men, even as we do toward you." There is no sweeter, purer love than that among Christians because it is God's love which flows through us to others, both Christians and non-Christians. Friendships, family love and humanitarian love are all more abundant and beautiful in the life of a Christian. What a blessing it is to be loved by Christian families and friends!

Grace—2 Corinthians 9:8: "And God is able to make all grace abound toward you; that ye, always having all sufficiency in all things, may abound to every good work." Only Christians can be sure that they will have "grace" (God's enabling power) so that they have all they need to "abound" in every good work. How comforting to know that God will give us more than enough power to do what we ought to do.

Thanksgiving—Colossians 2:7: "Rooted and built up in him, and stablished in the faith, as ye have been taught, abounding therein with thanksgiving." To "abound with thanksgiving," you must have a lot for which to be thankful! Psalm 68:19 says, "Blessed be the Lord, who daily loadeth us with benefits, even the God of our salvation." Learn to recognize and count your blessings daily, especially your salvation. The world is full of unappreciative people. Don't be one of them. Enjoy your abundant life!

TODAY'S PRAISE

I praise you, Lord, for not only giving me eternal life, but an abundant life now!

TODAY'S PRAYER

Father, help me to walk so close to you that my life will always abound with your blessings and provisions.

TODAY'S PROJECT

What other areas of the Christian life can you think of in which you can "abound"? List them. Also think of ways you can let the blessings of your life abound (flow over) to others.

JAN VAN HEE was saved as a teen and has always had a special burden and love for teenagers. She is a graduate of Bob Jones University, an accomplished conference speaker and writer, and is gifted in dramatic interpretation. She authored a Sunday School curriculum for young women, and for many years wrote the closing program for Neighborhood Bible Time. She started a club for teen girls and continued this ministry in each church she and her husband were called to serve. These clubs proved to be profitable in reaching young women as they learned everything from table manners to personal appearance to community service, all from a biblical perspective.

Jan and her husband Ron currently travel together as missionaries-at-large with Northwest Baptist Missions and as field representatives for Arabic Bible Outreach Ministries.

OTHER BOOKS BY JAN VAN HEE

No Turning Back: The Life and Adventures of Herbert Grings—Missionary to the Congo

Think on These Things, Challenging Thoughts for Teen Girls